Gulliver Travels Again:

A Journey to Find the Gulliver Ancestors

Susan E. Clarke

AuthorHouse™
1663 Liberty Drive
Bloomington, IN 47403
www.authorhouse.com
Phone: 1-800-839-8640

First published by AuthorHouse 07/06/2011

ISBN: 978-1-4389-6486-7 (sc)

Printed in the United States of America

Any people depicted in stock imagery provided by Thinkstock are models,
and such images are being used for illustrative purposes only.
Certain stock imagery © Thinkstock.

This book is printed on acid-free paper.

authorHOUSE®

Introduction

Gulliver Travels Again:

A Journey to Find the Gulliver Ancestors

Susan E. Clarke

THE STATELY HOMES OF ENGLAND

By Felicia Hermans. (1793–1835)

The stately homes of England

How beautiful they stand

Amidst their tall ancestral trees

O`er all the pleasant land.

(George Clarke`s favourite poem)

Contents

Foreword

Susan Clarke (my mum) had always told us who was who in our family past and present when we were children. She began to take notes on the family tree as soon as she could read and write, collecting the family's signatures in a little home-made book.

It wasn't until Susan developed a benign tumour and was expected to lose her eyesight in 1987 that she became determined to record it all and one day write a book.

She was passionate about researching her mother's side of the family, the Gullivers. The family came from a long line of farmers. Her grandfather, when dressed up in his pin-striped suit and bowler hat, looked every bit like a gentleman. He was treated by other farmers with great respect. And his surname was unusual – Gulliver.

As children we went with mum to the Birmingham library and the Delapré record office in Northampton and searched through books and reels of microfiche, noting down any records on scraps of paper.

At home there were folders with papers and notes that would have made no sense to anyone else. I think we all tried to help in various ways, but I don't think we had the passion or understanding of what mum was trying to achieve.

Then came the age of the Internet, and Susan became one of the first "silver surfers". Her research intensified, and notes were saved as computer files in some sense of order. It became her full-time hobby, as we had all left home and she could contact people and share information. If that wasn't enough, she appeared on television on the local news.

She even found time to teach young children how to start their family trees while working in a local middle school with disabled children.

Here is her book, written after extensive research over a period of years and after travelling to many parts of the country to meet new relatives and exchange information.

The book is Susan Clarke`s account of her journey looking for her grandfather's family.

Susie Brown

My Story

When I was a small girl in 1950s, my family would spend Saturdays on my grandparents' farm at Blisworth.

My grandfather, Fred Gulliver, was a quiet, hardworking gentleman who never spoke about his family.

The surname 'Gulliver' fascinated me!

I had heard of Gulliver's Travels, a story written by Jonathan Swift in the eighteenth century.

I was able to compile a family tree dating back to 1837 with comparative ease.

Charles Gulliver, my great-grandfather, had been a farmer and a lay preacher for the Methodist's, preaching in chapels in Eastcote, Litchborough, and Culworth.

My research started before computers were available. We took a journey to St Catherine's House in London. The records revealed that John Gulliver, my great-great-grandfather had farmed around Marston St Lawrence near Banbury.

Ancestors of John Gulliver had farmed land around Warkworth and Overthorpe near Banbury for hundreds of years. John Galover/Gulliver farmed in Warkworth and died in 1570.

One well-known Gulliver was George, who rose to become head of the College of Surgeons. Ancestors of his are buried in St Mary's churchyard in Banbury.

Did Jonathan Swift get the Gulliver name from here while visiting his relations in the area in and around Northamptonshire?

While visiting local libraries, we were able to read books on the history of Northamptonshire. They revealed that the old spelling of Gulliver had been Golafre or Goulafre. A gentleman, Phillip Kingston of Blakesley, confirmed this name was an old Norman name. A William Golafre came over with William the Conqueror and settled in England.

I had always looked up to my mother's family. They were middle class and well respected among the farming community. They were very careful with their money and spent it wisely.

My father's family didn't have much money since his ancestors were not able to read and write. One side of the Clarke family had been able to take advantage of the others in the family: the land and buildings at Blisworth, Northampton were signed over to the side of the family that could read and write. Sad to say, it wasn't my side of the family. My side were good honest hard-working people, living a frugal life style.

I felt at times that I was two people – from a working-class family, when looking at dad, and from the middle-class, when looking at my mother's side.

It all seems to have come together for me. After many years of research, I found connections to Jonathan Swift, Bram Stoker, Oscar Wilde, and Lillie Langtry.

It is the Gulliver/Golafre family.

Let me explain.

Way back, Robert le Breton (le Brito) married a Miss Phillipa Golafre (Gulliver), whose grandfather William Golafre had come over from Normandy with William the Conqueror and settled in Suffolk.

From a branch of the le Breton family came Emilie Charlotte le Breton (Lillie Langtry).

From the Golafre/Gulliver family came my mother's family, the Gullivers of Banbury and Northamptonshire.

A distant relation of the Gullivers of the Banbury area, Jonathan Swift, wrote a book called Gulliver's Travels.

Bram Stoker worked at the Lyceum Theatre in London and met Lillie Langtry with her lover, Edward Prince of Wales.

Lillie was best friends with Oscar Wilde.

Oscar Wilde's fiancée was Florence Balcombe.

Florence Balcombe married Bram Stoker.

Bram Stoker's second cousin was Gilbert Joseph Stoker of Dublin.

Gilbert Joseph Stoker is my granddaughter and grandson's third great-grandfather.

My mother always told me, `We are all related to one another.'

Yes, I think she is right.

Chapter One

The Gullivers of Northamptonshire

John Gulliver (born 1797) was my great-great-grandfather. He lived in Overthorpe near Banbury and was a farmer.

He was married to Joanna Middleton, who was born at Thenford, the village where Lord Heseltine lives.

John and Joanna Gulliver had a large family:

Thomas Gulliver (born 1823),

Ann Gulliver (born 1824),

Jesse Gulliver (born 1826),

Henry Gulliver (born 1830),

Mary Gulliver (born 1832),

Charles Gulliver (born 1834),

Ellen Gulliver (born 1836),

Eli Gulliver (born 1840).

Charles Gulliver (born 1834) was my great-grandfather. He was born in Marston St Lawrence and married Mary Heritage, daughter of Thomas Heritage. Together they lived in a beer house in West Thorp. Mary ran the beer house while Charles worked on the farm. They brought up eight children, though, sadly, one died. She was Susan Elizabeth (born 1868) and died at the age of seven from scarlatina.

I was probably named after Susan Elizabeth Gulliver.

I was born seventy-eight years later. I owe it to the Gullivers that all I know about them is written down for future generations to see.

Arthur Charles (born 1864) married Emma from Byfield. They had a large family of about eight children. Their youngest daughter was Ruby. My Aunt Nancy used to take us to visit her and her husband Les. They lived at the Magpie Farm, previously the Magpie Inn near Sulgrave. They didn't have any children. When Ruby died, her husband didn't want to live any more. The last time our family was to see him was at the farm sale at Glebe Farm, Blisworth, in September 1975. He later was found in his car with the engine running and the exhaust pipe attached into the car. He had committed suicide.

Magpie Farm was near Sulgrave Manor.

Sulgrave Manor had been the home of the Washington family, from which George Washington came. He became the first president of United States of America.

Edith Ann Gulliver (born 1865) married Mr Harry Darby. They had children.

Susan Elizabeth Gulliver (born 1867) died young.

Emma Gulliver (born 1870) worked at a big house in Surrey as a domestic servant for Mr and Mrs Sprott, who were ship-owners, before retiring to live with her sister Rosalie in the cottages at Foster Booth near Towcester.

Mary Gulliver (born 1872) was known as Aunt Poll. She married Mr Pithouse and lived at Towcester in Northamptonshire. She had a son, Sidney, and a daughter,

Doris. Sidney was very tall. When I met him in 1950, the old street gas lamps were being replaced in Far Cotton, Northampton, and new electric lights were being installed. My sister and I named the new electric light that was installed outside our house "Sidney" because it was so tall. Doris had the family trait of the pretty round face with dimples on the cheek. Some would say she was blessed by the angels! They both married and had children.

Rosalie (born 1874) was my favourite great-aunt. She was a nice and fun person to be around. She was tall and slim and was very much her own person. She was a lady who could see into the future and was very mystic. She was also pretty with a lovely smile, with dimples, but she never married. She enjoyed meeting people and writing letters, which is something I seem to have inherited. She loved animals and kept cats and ducks at the Gables cottages in Fosters Booth near Towcester. Rosalie and her sister Emma owned the four cottages.

Elizabeth (born 1879) married Eli Collins. They had children, and he worked as a clicker in a shoe factory in Northampton.

Fred (born 1881) was my grandfather and the youngest child.

When his father, Charles Gulliver, died in 1925 at Garlick Cottages, Foxley Farm near Blakesley, the family moved out and brought the four cottages at Fosters Booth. Three were let out to rent, and the two sisters lived in the middle one. My grandfather moved to Glebe farm in Blisworth with his wife Maria, née Watts, who was born in 1879

Their two children were

Nancy Mary Gulliver (born 1916, died 1992) and

Sylvia Joyce Watts Gulliver (born 1918, died 2008).

Glebe Farm

Glebe Farm, Towcester Road,

Blisworth, Northants, was built high on a hill. On a clear day you could see the lights of Northampton. When the motor racing was on at Silverstone, you could hear the cars roaring around the track.

The farm seemed to be a perfect place to be – within a short distance of the town, yet surrounded by fields and animals.

My grandparents and my Aunt Nancy lived on the farm.

My mother left the farm to get married in 1941 and moved away to Oxford. My father was transferred to work on the railway line at Oxford. His job was to see that the signal and telegraph were working during the Second World War. He was out in all weather, repairing the communication to keep the railway going.

After the war my parents returned to live in Northamptonshire. They brought a terraced house in Far Cotton, Northampton.

My sister and I were both born in the town. We had friends who were our near neighbours and friends from St Giles Church of England School in the town centre.

While we attended school during the week in the town, weekends and holidays were spent at Blisworth on the farm. We enjoyed visiting the farm and spending time with the animals. While there, we would help feed the lambs and the hens, while making sure we stayed out of the way of the cockerels. They liked to chase and attack us as we entered the hen house to collect the eggs. Sometimes we were allowed to bring the lambs into the farmhouse if they were small or poorly. There we would give them milk from an old medicine bottle with a special rubber teat on it.

When it came time for the lambs to have their tails cut, a farmer came to help out. Once they were sure that all the lambs were well, my grandfather or my aunty brought the tails into the kitchen of the farmhouse. Before we could eat the tails, they had to be singed with a flame until the wool had been burnt off the skin. They were then rubbed down and rolled in flour, before being cooked in a frying pan with lard. To eat them you could pick them up and hold them in your hand – a very nice tasty snack.

My grandfather kept cattle for beef, cows for milking, sheep for wool and mutton, hens for eggs, and cockerels for Christmas dinner.

He won awards for best cattle and root crop in Northamptonshire.

In the late 1940s he and my father went to Smithfield Market in London to see the Christmas Stock Show. There they met King George VI, the father of Queen Elizabeth II. The King asked my grandfather if he had any cattle in the show for sale. Fred Gulliver replied that, no, he didn't have any cattle in the show. With that the King moved on.

Later on, my grandfather acquired ducks from his sister Rose. She had kept them at the bottom of her garden and looked after them until she was ill and had to go into a nursing home in Newport Pagnell.

The ducks laid large white eggs with double bright yellow yolks.

When she died, she left everything to my grandfather.

In the front window of Rose's cottage were bright red geraniums. They had been brought from the farm at Foxley near Blakesley.

From there they were given to my grandma to look after at the farm at Blisworth. From her they passed to my mother and then to me. They must now be over one hundred years old. Yes, they are in my front window.

Nancy Gulliver never married. She was once engaged to a soldier. She had many friends, including men who would take her out to dinner. She always put the farm before men. She went out with my father before he married my mother. It seemed to us that we had two mothers – one for every day in the week and one for weekends and holiday treats.

My parents would take over the running of the farm for one week a year. This gave Nancy time away. She liked to get away from the farm for a break. Sometimes she would take my sister and me to Wales, Dorset, or Hampshire.

She was the one person we could talk to about anything. She was someone we looked up to, someone who was there for us.

We loved our mother, but she was like my grandfather, Fred Gulliver, a quiet person who didn't like a fuss.

Aunty Nan, as she was called, loved to meet people. She was able to do this, as part of her work was to take the produce from the farm and sell it locally.

After visiting Ruby and Les at the Magpie Farm, we carried on Sulgrave Manor, the former home of the Washington family. We had with us a very large basket of apples from the trees in the garden at Glebe Farm, Blisworth.

We were on our way to see the housekeeper of Sulgrave Manor;
the apples were for her.

The housekeeper allowed us to look at the manor from the outside and peer in through the windows. We were allowed a tour of the gardens. I was interested in old houses and their history.

Sometimes we were lucky to go out with our Aunty Nan on her rounds to sell or exchange fruit and vegetables with Young's Village Store in Blisworth. No cash changed hands. She would come away with flour and sugar and tea packed up into strong paper bags while we waited.

My grandmother stayed at the farm. She was busy working in the house and the dairy. She was the one who made butter from the cows' milk.

She would walk down the farm road and catch the bus to Towcester. In her basket was the butter wrapped up in greaseproof paper. When she arrived, she went to Newman's grocery store and handed the basket of butter over the counter and was paid.

As she got older and more disabled from Parkinson's disease, my Aunt Nancy took over her jobs as well as looking after her.

She allowed us to help churn the milk in the dairy until it separated into curds and whey. We would take it from the dairy into the kitchen and pat it into blocks. This was pure butter with no additives.

The family lived at Glebe Farm until Fred Gulliver died one afternoon in January 1975. He had his dinner in bed and then took an afternoon nap from which he never woke up.

Nancy moved to Harlestone to live with friends and work as a housekeeper. She lived out the rest of her life on a farm owned by Earl Spencer of Althorp. It was run by Ron and Barry Smith.

By this time, Sylvia (Joyce, as she liked to be called) and George Clarke were living in

Courteenhall Road, Blisworth.

There are many more families of Gullivers in Northamptonshire. They are all distant cousins of my grandfather.

In the 1700s and 1800s they had large families and began to lose touch with all their cousins. Only now in the twenty-first century with the help of computers have people started to take an interest again in genealogy. Years ago it involved a journey to reference libraries and record offices relevant to the town where the family had lived, and visits to graveyards.

Chapter Two

Althorp

We had grown up knowing about the Spencer family who lived at Althorp in Northamptonshire. On Sundays as children we attended All Saints Church in the centre of Northampton. It was a long walk from Far Cotton. We enjoyed the service and always sat upstairs in the church. On special occasions, the seventh Earl Spencer and his wife Lady Cynthia attended the church, and we had a full view of them from the gallery.

One of the times I touched royalty occurred in the 1980s.

I had been lucky enough to be taken round the Althorp house by a member of staff. The house was closed for the season, and the Spencer family were away.

Let me explain. After my grandfather died in 1975, my Aunt Nancy sold up the farm and moved to one of the farms that Earl Spencer owned. She became housekeeper to the farmer and his son.

At times they were invited to Althorp House for dinner to meet up with Earl Spencer, Princess Diana`s father. The farmer's son worked in London and helped out on the farm during his time off. Earl Spencer asked him to work part-time on the Althorp Estate.

He ran the wine shop there and was in regular contact with Earl Spencer. It was through this contact that we got to be shown round the house.

It was in the 1980s, and Diana and Prince Charles had just been married. There were celebrations at the house, and each person was given a piece of wedding cake. Aunt Nancy sent me a small piece by post. I kept it for many years until it disintegrated. Nancy was lucky to meet Princess Diana and Prince Charles and Prince William and Harry when they visited Althorp House.

My second daughter, Sarah, began to look more like Princess Diana as she grew up.

Sarah was a technician, working on the lighting for the show in which Paul O'Grady (Lily Savage) starred at Blackpool North Pier in 1990s.

While in Blackpool, she met the actor David Jason of Fools and Horses fame. He asked her if she would like to join a look-alike agency since he thought she looked like Princess Diana, but she declined. David Jason did arrange for her and her partner to have a small part in A Touch of Frost, in which he starred. It was later shown on television.

While working in London, Sarah was once mobbed by a coachload of Japanese tourists who thought she was Princess Diana. They shouted at her as they tried to take photos. Sarah didn't like being mistaken for the Princess; she tried to keep a low profile.

This got me thinking. If one of my daughters looked like Diana, maybe there was a family history connection.

I knew that one of Diana`s ancestors was Agnes Heritage.

The Heritages had been sheep farmers, as had my ancestors. My maternal great-great-grandmother was Mary Heritage before her marriage to Charles Gulliver. The family came from the same area just outside of Banbury just over the border in Warwickshire, near Wormleighton.

As I researched the family tree, at first I couldn't see any connection.

Yes, there was Susan Knightley and her brother Richard Knightley of Fawsley. Both had married into the Spencer family.

I left it for a while and hoped it would fall into place. After many hours of reading and researching, I did finally discover a connection.

William Knightley of Staffordshire married Dorothy Golafre/Golever.

(There are many spellings of the surname. It comes from an old Norman surname of Goulafre.)

The family had come over with William the Conqueror and settled in Suffolk.

After 1066 they began to change the spelling of the name until it became an English version of Gulliver.

Gulliver is the family name of my mother's family. I have traced them back in a direct line to 1580 in Banbury, Oxfordshire.

George Baker, in his book on Northamptonshire history, The History and Antiquities of the County of Northampton, issued in 1815, included many family genealogies. Among them I found the Golafre/Gulliver family dating back to the eleventh century, up to the fifteenth century. I still had more research to do.

Abington Abbey

As children growing up in Northampton, we were lucky to have so many green spaces to play in. We would be taken by our parents to Abington Park on a Sunday in summer time. We were allowed to play in the children's park and run up and down the hill near the manor house. After a walk round the lakes and by the trees where had stood the deserted village, we made our way back, visiting the peacocks and birds in the aviary and sitting on the grass and listening to the brass band. If we were good, we were allowed an ice cream.

The gardens were kept fully stocked with flowers and looked beautiful during the summer time.

Once a year the local drama club put on a play by Shakespeare that was performed in the grounds of the manor house.

The manor house had been home to Elizabeth Bernard, née Hall. She was the daughter of Susanna, née Shakespeare, and Dr Hall. Elizabeth was the granddaughter of William Shakespeare. On her death in 1669, the manor was sold to William Thursby. Elizabeth and her husband may be buried beneath the pews of Abington church of St Peter and St Paul.

Abington Park was first opened to the public in 1897. The house had been a gift from Lady Wantage, whose father, Samuel Jones Lloyd, was head banker for Jones, Lloyd, and Co., London. He became the first and last Lord Overstone.

Many times as children we were taken for a ride in my aunt's car. We travelled through the small country lanes in the summer time, taking a picnic with us. We would have bone china and a flask of tea, a medicine bottle filled with milk, lots of thick-cut sandwiches filled with egg or meat, and a home-made fruit cake to finish off with. Very often we would stop at the side of the road on the grass verge for the picnic. This was not far away from Foxley Farm, where my mother had been born and my great-grandfather and my grandfather had both farmed, and was nearby to Blakesley.

This was in the 1950s, and we could see Blakesley Manor standing in its own grounds.

Within a year or so it was demolished, a great historical building gone for ever.

Henry III had granted free warrant to all the land. It was given to William Plumpton, Peter Woddam, Peter de Stokes, and Hugh and Maud Golafre (Gulliver).

During Henry VIII's reign, the King gave the Manor of Blakesley to his daughter Princess Elizabeth, later to become Queen Elizabeth I. She stayed at the manor house during the time her palaces were being spring cleaned.

Blakesley

When we were children growing up in the 1950s in Northamptonshire, during weekends and school holidays Aunt Nancy enjoyed taking the whole family out in the motor car. There weren't many people who owned a car in those days, and the country roads were nearly empty, except for horses, carts, tractors, and land-rovers taking foodstuff and animals from and to the farms.

We didn't have a car. My father owned a bicycle, and later on he brought a Velocette motorbike that he used to get to work and for pleasure. I enjoyed many a motorbike ride with him, visiting small villages on the way. He wore the helmet and I wore a headscarf. We didn't realise the danger then of protecting our heads if we fell off. We were fortunate that we never did.

Most of our travel was done by bus or train. The latter was the best form of travel for me as I wasn't too good at travelling by road either by car or bus.

They were holding a jousting tournament in the grounds of Canons Ashby house. The house had been built on the site of an Augustan priory.

Canons Ashby had been the home of the Dryden family. Jonathans Swift's grandmother was Elizabeth Dryden; she was born at Canons Ashby. She married Thomas Swift and had two children, Jonathan and Thomas. Jonathan was the father of Jonathan Swift, the man who wrote Gulliver's Travels.

We watched the medieval jousting in the grounds of Canons Ashby. There were large crowds of people standing around the gardens. The tournament started; the knights came out in full armour, and the horses were in full dressage.

It was a very interesting afternoon. I enjoyed seeing the clothes and traditions of medieval times. As a child this excited me, and I wanted to know more of the lives of the people who lived in England during the Middle Ages.

Delapré Abbey

Our family had a few connections with Delapré Abbey in the twentieth century.

My mother's aunt, Elizabeth, née Watts, lived with her family in the small gatehouse on the London Road approach to the abbey. Her husband, Wills Mortimer, was gardener to the estate.

Previously they lived at Fawsley Hall Lodge, where he also was gardener.

Annie, Maria, Kate, and William Watts ,Elizabeth`s brother and sisters, followed her to live in Far Cotton Northampton.

Occasionally, my mother, sister, and I would be invited to tea with my mother's cousin, Aunt Ida. We really looked forward to seeing her. She would make cakes and sandwiches for us. She was a kind lady. She lived the gardener's cottage in the abbey grounds.

Her husband was head gardener and helper to Miss Bouverie, the owner of the house. She was in a wheelchair and need lots of help around the large house. In 1946 the Northampton Corporation purchased the estate. The people who had worked for Miss Bouverie were transferred to work for the council. They were moved out and given a council house at Hardingstone.

We lived in Euston Road in Far Cotton, and it was just a short walk from the abbey.

As we approached the farmyard gate, the geese came charging to the gate and made a loud honking noise. This alerted the owners of the house that someone was at the gate; there was no need for a guard dog.

We stood back and waited until someone came and moved the geese away.

I liked to walk round the gardens which were very well tended. There were apricot and peach trees growing on the garden walls.

The pond was filled with gold fish. The flowerbeds were brightly coloured, and the lawns immaculate. It was so peaceful away from the traffic.

If my father came with us, he liked to walk around the house and the grounds. My mother's cousin's husband Jim Fraser took my father to see the tunnel that runs underground from Delapré Abbey to All Saints Church in Northampton town centre. Jim had the keys to all the doors of the abbey and was able to unlock the door to the tunnel. Jim said that Miss Bouverie had told him that the tunnel had been used by the nuns to go to Northampton town centre and maybe to church at All Saints. Not many people have been lucky enough to see the tunnel. As children we weren't allowed there.

My father always dreamed of owning a big house. In 1958 or 1959, luck was on his side. A couple of ladies were selling a big old house in Blisworth. They were getting on in years, and the house was too much for them to handle. My father and most of his father's family had been in the village for over 300 years. We knew he would buy it and that our lives would change. We would not be living any more in the town of Northampton, but would become fulltime country people.

Fawsley Hall

In 1971 my children's father and I went to Fawsley Lakes. He went fishing, and I stayed by the lake side, knitting baby clothes for the baby I was soon to have. He brought me a root of water buttercups, beautiful bright yellow flowers from one of the lakes on the estate. I still have them in my garden pond, and every spring they come into bloom and remind me of Fawsley Hall and Lakes.

He had worked at the hall in 1950s, when it was used as a workshop for a timber company who leased the property.

My mother-in-law `s husband died in Northampton Hospital, and she moved away to Suffolk to be near one of her daughters. While sorting out her garden before she moved, she offered me a stone slab from her rockery. She told me that it had come from Fawsley Hall and was part of the building that had fallen down.

I can take a guess as to how it came to be in her garden. The slab of stone is now kept near my garden pond, a little bit of Fawsley in my garden.

Fawsley had started as a royal manor in the seventh century. The area was hunted by royalty from the nearby Anglo-Saxon palace at Weedon.

The Domesday Book states that the population of Fawsley was around fifty people.

In 1224 the King had granted the holding of a weekly market at Fawsley.

The Black Death wiped out between one third and half of the population but in 1377 there were 200 people living there.

The village was in the field surrounding the Church of St Mary's, Fawsley.

In 1066 the Knightley family came over from Normandy with William the Conqueror.

Some of them settled in the village of Knightley, Staffordshire.

In 1416 Richard Knightley became lord of the manor of Fawsley in Northamptonshire. He was a successful lawyer and sheep farmer.

The Knightley family owned thirty-three manors in Northamptonshire (according to Lady Louisa Knightley's book, The Journals of Lady Louisa Knightley).

The Knightley family changed the land they owned to use it for sheep farming, at the expense of the tenants, who were turned out of their homes by the fifteenth century.

Richard Knightley was twice Sheriff of Northamptonshire.

Sir Edmund Knightley was knighted in 1542. He held strong religious convictions. Once he tried to prevent King Henry VIII from taking the son of his deceased brother-in-law Sir William Spencer.

Susan Knightley married Sir William Spencer of Wormleighton in Warwickshire and Althorp House in Northamptonshire.

Sir William Spencer was the ancestor of the Spencer family of Althorp.

While Queen Elizabeth I's palaces were being cleaned, she would travel around the country and stay with well-to-do families at their houses.

In 1575 Queen Elizabeth was entertained at Fawsley. She stayed in the Queen's Chamber now renamed Suite 1575.

You too can stay at Fawsley Hall in the rooms where the Queen stayed.

The Victoria and Albert Museum had an exhibition called "The Decline of an English Country House". This showed how Fawsley was neglected after Lady Louisa Knightley died in 1913. She was the last Knightley to live at the hall.

Mr Saunders and his wife purchased the property in 1975, but due to financial problems they were unable to finish restoring it.

Work started again in 1996 with a consortium including Mr Saunders. Today it is a restored as a wonderful hotel.

Descendants of William Knightley and Dorothy Golafre

Dorothy Golafre is twentieth great-grandmother to Prince Charles, heir to the throne of England.

Dorothy was also twentieth great-grandmother to Diana, Princess of Wales.

Dorothy was fourteenth great-grandmother to George Washington, the first president of the United States.

Dorothy was eighteenth great-grandmother to Winston Churchill.

This information was taken from a website fabpedigree.com with permission from the owner.

William Knightley (born 1282) of Knightley Gnosall in Staffordshire

married Dorothy Golafre/Glover. (born 1270) of Gnosall, Staffordshire.

Roger Knightley (born 1329) of Gnosall married Sibil of Gnosall.

John Knightley married Elizabeth de Burgh of Burgh Hall, Staffordshire.

Richard Knightley married Elizabeth Giffard of Chillington.

Richard Knightley married Elizabeth Purefoy. They brought Fawsley Hall in Northamptonshire.

Richard Knightley (born 1417) married Eleanor Throckmorton (born 1424) of Bedfordshire.

Sir Richard Knightley married Jane Skennard.

Susan Knightley married William Spencer (died 1532).

Richard Knightley married Susan Spencer.

Brother and sister both married into the Spencer family of Althorp, Northamptonshire.

Sir John Spencer (died.1586) married Katherine Kitson.

Sir John Spencer (died 1599) married Mary Catlyn.

Their descendants include Charles Edward Maurice Spencer, the present ninth Earl Spencer of Althorp, Northamptonshire.

The late Diana Princess of Wales (born 1961) in Norfolk died in a car crash in Paris in 1997.

Diana`s two children are

Prince William (born 1982) and

Prince Harry (born1984).

Their father is Prince Charles, eldest son of Queen Elizabeth II.

Holdenby House

Originally, Holdenby House was built by Sir Christopher Hatton around 1570.
He was the son of William Hatton of Holdenby. He lived from 1540 to 1591 and was one of Queen Elizabeth I's favourites. He is buried in St Paul's Cathedral.
Following his death, the Holdenby estate was seized by the crown in lieu of debts.
In 1646–7 King Charles I was imprisoned there.
After the Restoration, the estate passed into the hands of the Dukes of Marlborough.
There was a disastrous fire at the house about 100 years later, leaving only the servants' quarters standing. These were refurbished, and the estate was purchased by William King, the husband of Rachel Gulliver. She was one of Brian Gulliver's great-great-aunts. Rachel and William's children erected a stained glass window above the altar in the estate church in memory of their parents. The estate was later purchased by Colonel John Lowther.
Written by Brian Gulliver of Cardiff, formerly of Wendover, near Aylesbury (died June 2006)

Hollowell Steam Fair

When I visited the Hollowell Steam Fair in Northamptonshire on
Sunday, 3 July 1994,

I couldn't escape the Gulliver name. In fact, there was even a steam tractor named Gulliver.
The present owners from Souldrop, Bedfordshire, brought the steamroller in the 1980s from the Gulliver family who lived at Church Farm, Souldrop. Church Farm was a farm of 100 acres. Among this family were Reg Gulliver, who brought the roller to use on the farm. He named it after his family, calling it Gulliver.
Reg and his two sisters and brother, Cecil, lived on the farm.
Cecil Gulliver was the local chronicle and echo weather man. He also worked for the meteorological office.
He studied the weather by looking at the clouds and kept a daily record of rainfall.
On the farm, Reg Gulliver reared bullocks. He was known for winning lots of prizes for exhibiting flowers and vegetables. When Reg died, his two sisters sold the steamroller. It was worth £50,000 in 1994.

The two sisters continued to live on the farm, keeping the house exactly as was fifty years ago. Aunt Nancy took us to visit them at the farm and have tea with them in the farmhouse. We enjoyed meeting more of the Gulliver family and found it very easy to talk to them about the family,

Northampton Castle

The Castle at Northampton was one of more than eighty castles built in William the Conqueror's time. The only remaining piece of the castle is the postern gate, which has been built into the Northampton (Castle) Rail Station wall.
Thomas à Becket was born in 1118 on Cheapside in London.
He had become friends with King Henry II. They often hunted together in the deer forests of Northamptonshire. Their route out of the town may have been through the wall gate near St Giles' Church in the town.
The two would attend church services at the castle church of St Peter's. This church had been restored by Simon de Senlis II. Sometimes they would attend the church of the Holy Sepulchres in Sheep Street, Northampton, where they could catch up on the news of the crusaders.
Thomas à Becket was taken to Northampton Castle and was put on trial in 1164.
He managed to escape and ran though the town. It is said he stopped for a drink at a well in the Bedford road.
The spring where it is said he drank from is called Becket's Well. The park opposite is called Becket's Park after this famous man. This park has the river Nene flowing through it.

Thomas managed to get to France and lived there until his return to England some years later. He was killed in Canterbury cathedral in 1170 by four men – Reginald Fitz Nurse, Hugh de Moreville (who held Knaresborough Castle), William de Tracy, and Richard Brito/Breton (the ancestor of Lillie Langtry).

After they had killed Thomas à Becket, they escaped to Knaresborough Castle near Harrogate.

They thought they were helping the King as he said he wished to be rid of the Archbishop Thomas à Beckett. Later, the four men went to meet the Pope, and he told them they had to stay in exile and fight for the Knights Templar in Jerusalem.

Richard Brito/Breton lived out the rest of his life in Jersey.

In 1213 Faulk de Breaute was made sheriff of many shires in the Midlands. He had married Margaret Redvers, née Fitzgerald. He asked the King's permission to marry Margaret, who was a widow. Her late husband, Baldwin de Redvers, came from the Earls of Devon.

Faulk held the title of Constable of Northampton Castle, and he and Margaret lived in the castle. They had one son, Thomas Breaute. He became an Oxfordshire county knight, a respectable man unlike his father. He held Upper Heyford Manor in 1255.

Margaret inherited many lands and manors across the country, including Vauxhall in London, Luton, and land in Yorkshire and the Isle of Wight. She was a very wealthy lady. Faulk was a nasty greedy man who worked for King John, gaining many manors and castles by force.

It was Margaret's grandmother, Matilda Golafre, whose family had lived in Northamptonshire at Blakesley.

Margaret's half-sister Joan de Cornhill married Hugh Neville. They lived at Leadenhall Manor in the City of London. The site is now Leadenhall Market.

Margaret had a son by Baldwin de Redvers, her first husband. His name was also Baldwin de Redvers. He married Amica de Clare, born in Usk, Monmouthshire in Wales, the daughter of Gilbert de Clare, Earl of Gloucester. They had two children. A son, Baldwin de Redvers, married Avis de Savoy from the Italian royal family. They had a son, John, who died young.

Baldwin de Redvers died before his sister Isabella, and all of his estates came to her.

Isabella de Redvers became Isabella de Fortibus on her marriage to William de Fortibus. Her title was Countess of Devon and Lady of the Isle of Wight.

Northampton Guildhall

From left to right,
the first-floor statues on the outside of the Northampton Guildhall are as follows;
St Thomas à Becket was tried at Northampton Castle in 1164 but escaped.
Queen Eleanor's husband, King Edward I, vowed that each place her coffin was rested on the journey to London from Lincoln, a memorial cross would be built. One was built at Hardingstone on the London Road.
Sir Thomas White (1492–1567) was born in Reading, Berkshire. He was
a sixteenth-century philanthropist who endowed a Northampton loan fund. He became
Lord Mayor of London, was an English cloth merchant, and founded St John's College, Oxford.
John Dryden
was born in Aldwinckle, Northampton in 1631. He was a poet and dramatist, related to Jonathan Swift who wrote the book Gulliver's Travels.
St Andrew is the patron saint of Scotland
St George is the patron saint of England
St Patrick is the patron saint of Ireland he may have been born in Northamptonshire at Bannaventa near Norton Daventry .

Richard I
granted the town its first existing charter (1189).
Henry II founded three orders of friars in Northampton.
His son Edmund Crouchback inherited many castles in England. His first wife was Aveline de Fortibus, great great great-granddaughter of Matilda Golafre of Northamptonshire.
Queen Victoria saw the guildhall built during her reign. She visited Northampton.
Henry VII
established a town council of forty men in 1489.
Edward IV
defeated Henry VI at the Battle of Northampton in 1460 near Hardingstone.
St Michael is the patron saint of corporations.

Chapter Three

Banbury

Ride a cock horse to Banbury Cross
To see a fine lady on a white horse.
With rings on her fingers and bells on her toes,
She shall have music wherever she goes.

This nursery rhyme may refer to Celia Fiennes. Born in 1662, she travelled to many counties of England on horseback, either with relatives or with one or two servants. She wrote a book about her travels and the things she had seen, Through England on a Side Saddle in the Time of William and Mary. Her grandfather was William Fiennes, First Viscount Saye and Sele, who lived at Broughton Castle near Banbury.

Celia describes Banbury as a pretty little town in her book.

We had visited Banbury many times. The Gullivers had been aldermen of Banbury and owned shops and public houses. They also farmed in the area around Banbury town.

There are graves of the Gullivers in St Mary's Church graveyard.

I can remember when Aunt Nancy took us all in the black Ford car to Banbury for the day. We were squashed in the back seat together. My aunt was driving, and grandfather was sitting in the front seat. My mother and sister and I were in the back. There were no seat belts in those days, and we were so close together we couldn't move.

My grandfather had cattle for sale at the Banbury market that was held in the town. He wanted to see what price they would fetch. We left him at the market and walked around the town centre.

The old town centre had once been compact with many small shops.

Over the years the town has expanded, and houses and businesses were built on what was previously farm land. At that time, the museum was near to Banbury Cross; today it is housed at Castle Quay shopping centre, near to the canal and railway.

The visit had to include a trip to the Old Cake Shop in Parsons Street. It was here that the Banbury cake used to be made. Now the Banbury cake can be purchased from shops or coffee shops or from the museum and tourist centre in Banbury or by post via the Internet. The cake consists of puff pastry filled with currants, brown sugar, dried fruit spices, and rose water. Banbury cakes are usually sold in threes and are best eaten warm.

It is known that Edward Prince of Wales, the eldest son of King George V and Queen Mary, was sent some and enjoyed them.

Princess Diana's great-grandfather Earl Spencer was also sent Banbury cakes and wrote a letter of thanks saying how much he had enjoyed eating them.

Information on Banbury cakes can be found on Philip Brown's website, www.banburycakes.co.uk.

BROWN'S ORIGINAL BANBURY CAKES.

The name of Brown, more specifically E.W.Brown, has been directly associated with The Original Banbury Cake since 1868. Indirectly through family connection, the association goes back to 1818, when Samuel Beesley, a quaker, purchased the business in Parson's Street, Banbury, from the successors of Betty and Jarvis White, famous local bakers of their time.

The Original Cake Shop, as depicted in the Registered Trade Mark, was built circa 1550 but evidence of an earlier bakehouse went back to the early C13th.. This would correspond to the time when dried fruit and spices were brought back to these shores from the Near East by the crusaders, and where it is believed the origins of these cakes lie. They were widely used as celebration cakes at gatherings and feasts and were highly regarded as a delicacy.

After the death of Samuel Beesley in 1843 the business was let to the Lamb family, quakers from Sibford nearby Banbury, who ran it until 1868 when Wilks Brown, a quaker and woollen draper from Warrington, purchased the business for his wife Elizabeth(nee West), and their two daughters Elizabeth and Charlotte.

Elizabeth and Charlotte Brown, nieces of Samuel and Deborah Beesley continued to run the business and were subsequently joined by their nephew, Wilfrid E.A.Brown in 1929. His son Philip joined the firm in 1966 and helped to run it until his father retired in 1983.

These cakes are made from Brown's Original Recipe and contain the finest ingredients: Wheat flour,vegetable fat, butter,finest Greek currants and other fruit, Cane Sugar, spices and natural flavourings.

Philip Brown has recreated these cakes in their traditional form. We sincerely hope you enjoy them.

The Registered Trade Mark and recipe is owned solely by Philip Brown.

Celia Fiennes Genealogy

Celia Fiennes (born 1662; died 1741) was
born in Salisbury. She was a travel writer.
She spent her time riding side saddle on a horse around the country.
As she travelled on her journey around England, she was accompanied by relatives or servants and stayed with friends or family in their homes before travelling on.
Her great-great-grandparents were
Susan Knightley of Fawsley, Northamptonshire and her husband William Spencer.
Her great-grandparents were
Susan Spencer and her husband John Temple of Stowe, Buckinghamshire.
Her grandparents were
Elizabeth Temple of Stowe and William Fiennes (died 1662).
Her parents were
Nathaniel Fiennes and Frances Whitehead,.

Ranulph Fiennes

The Knightley and Spencer families appear in the genealogy of Celia Fiennes.
Again I find that a minute trace of Golafre blood has trickled through, this time to Celia Fiennes.
I am very proud of the Gulliver/Golafre family. Yes, I know that their name isn't written everywhere. But their descendants are quite famous.

I wrote a letter to Sir Ranulph Fiennes congratulating him on his successful climb of Mount Everest.
He replied with a letter and photographs of himself on Mount Everest. One was personally signed, "To Susan with best wishes, Ran Fiennes, 2009".
He was interested in my family tree and that I had read Celia Fiennes' travel book. She is one of his ancestors. Members of the family still live at Broughton Castle near Banbury.
They include Nathaniel Fiennes, the twenty-first Baron Saye and Sele.
The film Shakespeare in Love was filmed at the castle in 1998. It starred Joseph Fiennes, a cousin of Ranulph Fiennes.

Fyfield

In 956, Fyfield came into the possession of the Abbey of Abingdon.

Six hundred years later in 1555, Sir Thomas White, the founder of St John's College, Oxford, endowed the college with his Fyfield manor. Sir John Golafre had lived in the manor. He was a brother of the Abington Guild of the Holy Cross. He helped towards the cost of building the Abington Bridge in 1416.

During our visit to Fyfield, we were on able to borrow the large key to unlock the church door from a lady in village.

Inside the church can be seen the Golafre chapel. There is a large table tomb of Sir John Golafre. The lower slab shows Sir John Golafre as a skeleton figure, reminding us that when we die we cannot take anything with us. The north aisle of the church was made into the chantry chapel.

Looking around the church, I was surprised that there were not any stained glass windows. There had been a fire in 1893, and it destroyed much of the church.

Across the village green stands the manor house built in the fourteenth century where Sir John Golafre lived.

The manor house was let to Blackwell's book business, and they stored their old books there. An employee of Blackwell's served as caretaker and lived in the manor. When we visited, he was away on business. However, we did correspond, and I was invited to a tour of the manor – something I have not been able to do.

After Blackwell's book business moved out, the house was occupied by an heiress of Heinz (the baked beans company). I am not sure who lives there now.

Large wooden gates were locked to preventd us from entering the grounds of the manor, but I was able to look over the wall and take a photograph.

Further along the village is the White Hart Restaurant. It is a fourteenth-century former chantry house. Today it is a local pub and successful restaurant run by Mark and Kay Chandler.

Margaret Golafre of Fyfield

Margaret was a daughter of John Golafre, who owned the manor of Fyfield.

Margaret married first Fitzalan and secondly John de la Pole. His mother, Elizabeth of York, was in direct line to the throne of England. Her brother was King Edward IV. He had married Elizabeth Woodville of Grafton Regis in Northamptonshire.

Their two sons Edward V and Richard Duke of York were locked away in the Tower of London.

King Richard lost his only son, and John de la Pole was the next in line for the throne of England.

Had he lived, he would have been King John and Margaret Fitzalan, née Golafre, would have been Queen Margaret. John de la Pole was killed at the battle of Stoke. It was mentioned in the book on the History of Fyfield, but the author had not understood the connection to the royal family.

John de la Pole's grandmother was Alice Chaucer, granddaughter of the poet Geoffrey Chaucer.

Wytham

After visiting Fyfield, we drove to the village of Wytham.

This village is between three and four miles from Oxford. It has been used many times for the filming of the Inspector Morse TV series, starring the late John Thaw.

The church was locked, and we were unable to view inside. We continued on our journey home a little disappointed.

It was in Wytham that Juliana Golafre lived after her marriage to Robert Wytham.

They are both buried in the small village church.

Oxford

A trip around the city centre of Oxford revealed many old buildings. On approaching the Westgate Shopping Centre, we found a dismal modern building constructed of concrete. It was opened in 1972 and contains shops that are common to most towns. Beneath the shopping centre lie the remains of the monastery. This was built by the Greyfriars.

Sir John Golafre and his uncle Thomas Golafre of Quainton near Aylesbury, who died in 1378, were both buried there.

When the archaeologists unearthed the remains of the bodies of people buried there, they were removed to another burial site in Oxford.

A written report from the archaeologists was sent to the management of Sainsbury's, before planning and building permission was granted to build the shopping centre.

Chapter Four

Burnham Beeches

A day out by coach had been organised from Blisworth. It may have been through the women's institute, or perhaps it was the church choir outing. I was excited about the day out to Burnham Beeches.

Burnham Beeches! Great, I thought, we are going to the sea side! Before too long we arrived. There was no sea or sand in sight, just rows of beech trees in autumn colours of leaves fallen on the ground.

We were in Buckinghamshire, the next county to Northamptonshire, just a few miles away.

The adults enjoyed seeing the trees. The junior members of the group were a little disappointed. We wandered around the woods, waiting until the grown-ups were ready to get back on the coach.

The beeches have been used in many films, including the Carry-On films, Harry Potter and the Order of the Phoenix, and also Robin Hood.

Not known to me at the time but further on was the village of Burnham with its church and small abbey.

Sir John Golafre

Sir John Golafre of Quainton, Buckinghamshire died 1397. He was married twice to Amice de Langley and to Isabella Brocas but had no children.

He did have two children with his mistress, Joan Pulham.

Sir John Golafre (junior) is buried in Westminster Abbey. He was

Governor of

Jersey, Guernsey, Alderney, Brecqhou, Herm, Jethou, and Sark in the Channel Islands. He was also

Constable of Wallingford Castle in Oxfordshire and

Captain of Brest in Brittany. France.

Alice Golafre became Prioress of Burnham Abbey near to Burnham Beeches.

All my life it seems that I have had a desire to visit many parts of the country where the Golafre family had lived.

Stowe Gardens

We visited Stowe Gardens in 2009.

I was really looking forward to the visit. My last visit in 1997 had been a short one. This time I had won a free entry ticket for two from the National Trust. My visit was with a cousin. We both enjoyed going round the gardens so peaceful and well maintained.

We walked by the English Worthies, statues of well-known English people including William Shakespeare. We sat and looked at the wonderful views, and we walked to the Palladian Bridge. To me it was a peaceful place to be.

Looking out over land that had belonged to the Temple family, I imagined Peter Temple and his family walking round the gardens and marvelling at all the beauty surrounding them.

Peter Temple had first leased the land in Stowe. Later on he purchased it from the money he made as a successful sheep farmer. In the National Trust leaflet the gardens have been described as a piece of heaven. Birds and ducks and sheep and lots of green land and trees, with monuments and statues dotted around the park, completed the picture. The sun shone, and the day was enjoyable. The gardens are owned by the National Trust and are open to the public. The house is a public school and is run by Stowe preservation trust. It can be viewed at certain times.

Peter Temple's son John married Susan Spencer from Everdon in Northamptonshire. They lived at Stowe. She was the eighth great-granddaughter of Dorothy Glover/Golafre and William Knightley. Again the name of Golafre died out, but their descendants married well.

Stratford-upon-Avon

During the 1980s, we decided to have a day out from our town of Rugby in Warwickshire and visit Stratford upon Avon, the birth place of William Shakespeare.
Stratford has a beautiful large park leading down to the River Avon. There is plenty of car parking space and room to have a picnic on a nice warm day. On the opposite side of the river is the theatre. Further along is the Church of the Holy Trinity where William Shakespeare is buried. In the church is a bust of Shakespeare, and below the ground is the grave of the great playwright.

Men were enjoying themselves fishing from the banks of the Avon.
To get to the other side we used the service of a small boat pulled by a chain across the river. After we had allowed the children to let off steam, we ventured into town. There were lots of

people – mostly tourists from America. They had come to see where William Shakespeare was born and lived and was buried.

I marvelled at the old buildings still standing. Outside each one long queues of people were waiting to go inside. We walked around the old town, past his birthplace in Henley Street, his old school, and the museum.

Nash House was once the home of Thomas Nash and William Shakespeare`s granddaughter Elizabeth Hall.

She was later to live at Abington Manor in Abington Park, Northampton.

We passed by Hall Croft, the home of his daughter Susanna and her husband Dr John Hall. At the side of the house we could see a beautiful garden full of flowers and herbs. Dr Hall used to grow herbs to treat his patients.

William Shakespeare's mother was Mary Arden, the daughter of Robert Arden, a yeoman farmer from Wilmcote.

She was her father`s favourite child. In his will he left her the Wilmcote estate. The Arden family has been described by Dugdale as `the most ancient and worthy family'.

William`s father, John Shakespeare, was a glover and a wool merchant.

I had visited Birmingham Library – a vast library housed in a modern building with miles of shelves of books. The library had been opened in 1974, and it holds a special section on Shakespeare. It was there I was to find his family tree. The librarian fetched me a copy of records containing the Heralds' Visitations of Warwickshire. From this I learned that the Arden family had descended from Beatrix Golafre. She is described as "sister and heir of William Golafre, descending from Sir John Golafre of Sarsden, Oxfordshire".

As of 2010, a new library is being constructed near the Repertory Theatre in Birmingham. It is hoped that the new library will be opened in 2013.

Roger Golafre.

Beatrix Golafre (born. 1350) of Satley, Warwickshire married John de Clodshale.

Richard Clodshall (1384) married Elizabeth Edgbaston.

Elizabeth Clodshall married Robert Arden (born 1413) of Park Hall.

Walter Arden married Eleanor Hampden (1445–1525).

Thomas Arden (1469) married unknown.

Robert Arden (1506–1557) married Mary Webb (born 1512).

Mary Arden (1537–1608) married John Shakespeare.William Shakespeare married Anne

Hathaway.
Susanna Shakespeare married Dr John Hall.
Elizabeth Hall   married first Thomas Nash and second Sir John Bernard.

Roger Golafre was Mary Arden`s fifth great-grandfather.
Therefore, Roger Golafre became William Shakespeare`s sixth great-grandfather.
William Shakespeare's daughter Susanna married Dr John Hall and lived in Stratford upon Avon.
They had three children, Susanna, Hamnet, and Judith, who were twins. Hamnet died of the plague. Judith married Richard Quinney. They had three children, but none survived.
Susanna first married Thomas Nash. Her next marriage was to Sir John Bernard . They didn't have any children.
Their home was Abington Manor .Abington Park. Northampton.

Chapter Five

Westminster Abbey

We had visited Westminster Abbey with a view to finding the tomb of Sir John Golafre. We were told that he was buried in the Chapel of St Nicholas. We walked around the Abbey. There are nine chapels including St Nicholas' Chapel. We entered the chapel but were disappointed to find that his tombstone had been broken. Pieces of the stonework had been saved and placed in the Abbey store room for safe keeping.

A number of names from this genealogy are buried in St Nicholas' Chapel .

Sir John Golafre was

Constable of Wallingford Castle, Oxfordshire (died 1396).

Phillipa de Mohun was
Duchess of York and Lady of the Isle of Wight. She died in 1431 at Carisbrooke Castle in the Isle of Wight and is buried in the Chapel of St Nicholas. Her gravestone is intact. She was married three times, first to Sir Walter Fitz Walter (died 1386), second to Sir John Golafre with whom she had no children, and third to the Duke of York (died 1415).

The research had not been done on Princess Aveline at the time of the visit to the Abbey. So it wasn't until many years later that I was able to piece the family tree together.

Aveline de Fortibus was the daughter of Isabella de Fortibus, Lady of the Isle of Wight and great-granddaughter of Matilda Golafre of Northamptonshire.

She was the last living child of Isabella and her husband William de Fortibus.

She married Edmund Crouchback, the first Earl of Lancaster and son of King Henry III.on April 8th 1269 They were the first couple to marry in Westminster Abbey after the building had been completed.

Aveline de Fortibus became Princess Aveline on her marriage to Prince Edmund and became a member of the royal family. She died in 1273 aged fifteen. The couple had no surviving children. They were both buried in Westminster Abbey.

Edmund Crouchback was the first Earl of Lancaster. He was Prince Edmund, the son of King Henry III and Eleanor of Provence.

His first marriage was to Aveline de Fortibus, and his second was to Blanche of Artois. They had four children –
Thomas, Henry, John, and Mary.

The House of Lords

It was 30 October 2008.

It had been 403 years and 6 days since some of my distant ancestors had tried to blow up the Houses of Parliament, but here I was being invited to the Palace of Westminster.

Little did the authorities know that I was related through Margaret Golafre, to Robert and Thomas Winter.

Margaret was related to Sir John Golafre from Fyfield, formerly in Berkshire, but now in Oxfordshire.

Margaret had married John Huddington of Worcestershire.

Her sixth great-grandsons were Robert and Thomas Winter (Wintour).

They were found guilty and executed in London along with Robert Keyes, their cousin, and Guy Fawkes.

Thomas Winter helped organise the unsuccessful plot. Thomas and Robert, his brother, helped dig the tunnel under the House of Lords.

Thomas Percy knew of people in parliament and was able to rent a cellar under the House of Lords to store barrels of gunpowder. However, a letter was sent to Lord Monteagle, and the authorities were informed.

Robert Winter with others was tied to a wooden rack and dragged through the streets of London to St Paul's Churchyard and executed.

Thomas Winter (1571–1606), Robert Keyes, and Ambrose Rookwood were hung, drawn, and quartered in 1606 at Old Palace Yard in Westminster.

We passed by there on our way to the Black Rod Entrance. I wasn't there to carry out such an awful deed.

My outing was by invitation to the House of Lords. I had received a letter from Relate Centre Office, London.

Relate were celebrating seventy years as a relationship counselling charity.

My name had been put forward as an "unsung hero", due to my volunteer work for the past fifteen years as a receptionist.

Ian, the operations manager of Relate in Northampton, accompanied me. We had to go through very high security with everything x-rayed, and we had to carry a photo of ourselves. We were given badges with our names on. On my badge was written "unsung hero". I spoke to a lady from Oxfordshire who also had a similar badge.

She had worked as a volunteer for Relate for about eighteen years. We met up with Denise Knowles, a Relate counsellor who has appeared on television and radio.

There were many speeches by members of the head office of Relate.

We were given fruit juice or wine and a selection of canapés.

My journey there had been by train and taxi. The taxi-driver had tried to take a short cut across London by going by the back streets of Covent Garden.

Roadwork was in progress, and London was like a large traffic jam, with no one going anywhere. We arrived at the House of Lords late.

The men involved in the Gunpowder Plot had ridden on horses to London. This would have been a very long tiring journey into London.

Mine had been comparatively easy.

Leadenhall Market

The Front of Leaden-Hall.

In 1309, Sir Hugh Neville and his wife Joan de Cornhill set up home in a large mansion in Leaden Hall in the City of London. The house was so called because the roof was covered with lead.

Joan was the daughter of Alice de Courcy, half-sister to Margaret Fitzgerald. Their maternal grandmother was Matilda Golafre. Their grandfather was William de Courcy.

Sir Hugh Neville was known as Farmer Hugh. He allowed ordinary people to set up market stalls in his large back garden to sell their produce.

This was the start of Leadenhall Market.

By 1397 the market sold meat, fish, and cheese, along with other food.

In 1408 the lease of the manor of Leadenhall was given to Richard Whittington, known as Dick Whittington of the famous pantomime Dick Whittington and His Cat.

The City of London was given the freehold of the manor in 1411.

Part of the market was destroyed by the Great Fire of London. It has been rebuilt many times.

The present Victorian market was designed by the architect Horace Jones.

The market was used in the film Harry Potter and the Philosopher's Stone.

Vauxhall

Warin Fitzgerald had been hereditary chamberlain to the king. Margaret Fitzgerald, the daughter of Warin and Alice, née Courcy, married Baldwin de Redviers. When Baldwin Redviers died in 1216, his wife was not allowed to mourn for him. Within seven weeks King John had found her another husband, Faulk de Breauté, the Sheriff of Oxford. He was given the manor of Luton and was a favourite of the king. Margaret wasn't ready to marry again but was forced into it. He knew that Margaret was heiress to a vast fortune and wanted some of it for himself. They lived for a time in Northampton Castle.

Faulk was a very violent man. He had beheaded a deacon, plundered the town of St Albans, murdered a servant of the abbey, burnt houses, destroyed parks of many noblemen, and destroyed St Paul's Church in Bedford.

After his marriage to Margaret he kept having bad dreams of a large stone falling on him from St Alban's Abbey.

This never happened, but karma was working on him for all the bad he had done.

Faulk's Hall in Lambeth was the property of Margaret and Faulk. The name was changed, and it became known as Vauxhall in 1661. The grounds were opened as a large public garden until 1859. The land was used to build a factory called Alexander Wilson that making marine engines. Later this firm changed its name to Vauxhall Iron Works. This was the beginning of the Vauxhall car industry. The firm were later moved to Luton to produce cars. This has now ceased, but they still produce vans.

Dick Whittington

Richard Whittington lived from 1350 to 1423. He was born in Gloucestershire, the youngest son of Sir William Whittington who died 1358.

The eldest son inherited the estate, while the younger ones had to find fame and fortune where they could. It was hoped that the daughters would marry into wealthy families.

It is recorded that Richard (Dick) Whittington had two brothers, Sir William Whittington (born 1265; died 1284) and Dr Robert Whittington, the surgeon to the throne. He married Cecily

Browning . Their son was Sir Guy Whittington 1390 married and had eight children.
 Robert Whittington, the eldest, married and had three children.
Dick Whittington came to London to find work. He found it with a merchant named Ivo Fitzwarren (or Warin) from Wantage in Berkshire, though it is now in Oxfordshire. Fitzwarren had a daughter named Alice, and Dick fell in love with her.

SIR RICHARD WHITTINGTON,
Thrice Lord Mayor of London.

My favourite pantomime was Dick Whittington and His Cat. I grew up thinking that the story of Dick Whittington was a fairy story, not realising it was based on a true story.

The pantomime is based on the story that Dick did have a cat and that his family were poor. The latter is not true, as his family were quite well off, but he may well have had a cat. There were so many mice and rats in London that it would have been an asset to have a cat to kill the vermin.

In the story, Dick was given the attic of Fitzwarren's house to sleep in. Perhaps he did have a cat and it killed the mice and rats while he slept.

Fitzwarren asked his servants to put money towards a sailing voyage. Dick had no money to spare, but he did offer his cat. The captain of the ship took the cat to kill the rats on the ship and protect the goods there from being destroyed. The king heard about the cat and paid Dick a huge sum of gold to buy the cat. Dick became a wealthy man. He was able to marry Alice. Sadly they never had any children.

In real life, Richard Whittington became Mayor of London three times – in 1397, 1406, and 1419.

He died in London and was buried in the churchyard of St Michael Paternoster. The church was destroyed in the Great Fire of London. Later a new church was built called St Michael Paternoster Royal. Inside this church there is a stained glass window dedicated to Richard Whittington, Lord Mayor of London.

Juliana Golafre was the daughter of Sir John Golafre of Blakesley, Northamptonshire, and Sarsden and Lady Elizabeth of Fyfield. Juliana married Robert Wightam of Witham in Berkshire. They had one son, Richard de Witham, and seven daughters. Richard Witham married Alice Daundeney. It was one of their daughters, Agnes, who married a William Browning who died

1444. This made a connection with the Golafre family through the Wighthams of Witham and the Brownings to the Whittington family. The Brownings were connected with the manor of Leigh and Notgrove Manor in Gloucestershire.

Cardiff

I was on my way to visit Cardiff to meet my new found cousin, Brian Gulliver.

He had found me through an article in our local newspaper, the Chronicle and Echo. It was a report on my research into William Shakespeare's ancestors and our family connections.

We met at Cardiff rail station. I knew him from a photo he had sent me of himself. He was small in height but with a big appetite for family history. He was a real gentleman and treated me very well. We had so much in common and were able to finish one another's sentences.

It was pleasant to meet a distant cousin who was interested in genealogy. We went out to lunch at a country park. Afterwards we walked and talked all the time about our families. He told me that the Gullivers on his side of the family had moved to London and had connections with a paint factory in London. There was also some association with the AA car breakdown company.

I was invited to stay at his bungalow and meet his two married sons. I was given the bedroom with the en suite bathroom. During the night, a lady appeared at the end of the bed. It was his late wife. She said to me that she would like Brian and me to be the best of friends. In the morning I told him about his late wife appearing at the end of the bed. He wasn't surprised that she had appeared to me. We were the best of friends until his death twelve years later. Every Sunday evening he would phone for one hour, and most of the talk would contain the name Gulliver .

We would give each other a task to do the following week. It was his dream that a book would be written on the Gulliver family and that he would one day live in one of the Gulliver manor houses. This book, I hope, partially fulfils his and my dream. Sadly, he did not live to see it happen.

For my mother's eightieth birthday celebrations in 1998, I held a party at my home. I invited Tom Gulliver, John Gulliver, and Brian Gulliver, cousins of my mother. This was the first and last time they were to meet. There were three generations of the Gulliver family present. My mother, my sister and I, and both of us had some of our children there. I invited the local newspaper, the Chronicle and Echo, to come and take photographs and write a report of the day. They turned up and made the day very special for all of us.

We had traced our family trees back to the Gullivers from Banbury. Brian`s family had owned shops and public houses in Banbury and a brewery in Aylesbury. My family had been farmers at nearby Overthorpe, Banbury.

The London Palladium

On returning home from Cardiff, I searched the Internet for either a paint factory or the AA in London, instead I found information on Charles Gulliver. It was recorded on Matthew Lloyd's website www.arthurlloyd.co.uk.

This is a very interesting website on the history of the theatres in the British Isles. Matthew has done lots of research. He is the great-grandson of Arthur Lloyd, an entertainer, playwright, and baritone singer.

Rotherhithe Hippodrome opened 1899 and was demolished in 1955. It had been damaged in World War II.

In 1923 the premises closed and a receiver was appointed. It opened under the ownership of Charles Gulliver.

It seemed that Charles Gulliver had moved from Southampton to London. He first started work in a solicitor's office and later became first secretary of the Automobile Association. He went on to become Managing Director of London Theatres of Variety, owning over thirty music halls, including the London Palladium.

He brought a house, Morewenstow in Wallington, Surrey. He later sold it, and it became Collingwood School. This school was owned first by Mrs Hollis and then Mr Ingham.

Charles Gulliver moved to Bexhill-on-Sea and was interested in the game of bowls. He wanted to form a private bowls club. Land was chosen between Cantelupe Road and Knowle Road in Bexhill; it was originally known as Cantelupe Gardens. In 1951 the land was purchased and Knole Park (Bexhill) Ltd was floated on the stock market. The directors were Charles Gulliver, his son Clifford, and three nephews, Harold, Ronald, and Reginald.

St Pancras Station

On a rainy day in January 2008, I ventured into London on a train. It is not a place I like to stay for more than a day at a time. The city is so busy with people and taxis and buses everywhere. There is no time to stop!

I wanted to see the newly restored St Pancras rail station. What a splendid building it is, keeping the old building and combining the new extension to house the Eurostar trains, which have been transferred from Waterloo Station in London. Inside the station is like a travelling palace fit for royalty, yet full of people from all over the world – a new gateway to the world!

The building had been designed by Sir George Gilbert Scott, born at Gawcott in Buckinghamshire, the son of the local vicar. He designed many buildings, including Rugby School and the master's houses.

His son, Sir Giles Scott, designed the old red telephone box that is so typically British.

I first went to see St Pancras old church. A large part of the graveyard was removed when St Pancras rail station was built.

Among the gravestones was that of Mary Shelley's mother. Later her remains were removed to Bournemouth. A gravestone in the shape of the first British telephone box stands in the middle of the churchyard. It is said that Giles Scott got the idea of the shape from the gravestone. An old tree stands with many headstones planted around its roots. These were removed from the half of the graveyard, where the remains of bodies were dug up to make room for the St Pancras rail station. Under the present extended station buildings runs the diverted River Fleet, encased by the station.

After half a day spent looking around the station and admiring the new statue of two people meeting or saying goodbye designed by Paul Day, it was time for me to leave. Unable to see a bus-stop, I stood in a queue and waited. It was a taxi rank – an expensive way of returning to Euston Station.

In front of me was a McDonalds fast-food establishment. Not known to me at the time, the building had been occupied in 1861 by Doctor Edwin T. Watkins. He was born at Towcester, Northamptonshire, and moved to 21 Euston Road, Camden, London with his family and servants. Included among the servants was Mary Heritage, my great-grandmother. She was cook at 21 Euston Road for the whole family. I remember my Aunt Nancy telling me that her grandmother Mary Heritage, later to become Mary Gulliver, had been a very good cook. It all fitted together; cooking is something that has passed down through the family.

Mary Heritage was cook for a doctor and his family.

Emma Gulliver (a cook), Mary`s daughter, lived at Cobham Surrey.

Nancy Mary Gulliver was a good cook who worked at Hervey's Cottage in Weston Favell, Northampton.

Susan Clarke, the author, was a cook at Stanley House, Rugby School.

Jenny Mary Austin, née Clarke, Susan's youngest daughter, was a chef trained at Northampton College.

Chapter Six

Suffolk

My journey to Suffolk in 1999 was by train, my favourite mode of travel. I had found out that my ancestors had first lived in Suffolk after coming over in 1066 with William the Conqueror.

Arriving in Ipswich, I travelled by car to Halesworth, where I was to stay for a few days. I was staying with my children`s father. This would be the centre to go out from and explore the Suffolk countryside with its winding narrow roads and pink-coloured cottages along the way. But we had to look out for the very large tractors that used the roads to get to the farms where they worked.

During a visit to the local studies library in Lowestoft, I was showed copies of Walter Arthur Copinger's book The Manors of Suffolk. The Golafres/Gullivers had been given many manors by William the Conqueror. There were too many papers to read, so I had them photocopied for me to bring home and study.

Dunwich

As I always liked to see the sea, one day was spent at Dunwich, a town that was lost to the sea in the thirteenth or fourteenth century.

The churches of Dunwich have disappeared into the sea . The Church of St Felix, a cell of the Priory of Eye, was among the first to disappear. It is said by historians that the bells of the church can be heard at certain times, way under the sea.

The graveyard of All Saints Church has fallen over the cliff into the sea. A member of my family has seen a skeleton overhanging the cliff. Everything is calm for now, but there is a feeling that the sea will claim more of the land and take the rest of Dunwich with it.

All that remains now is a small village, though it is still called the town of Dunwich. On the cliff are the remains of the rebuilt Greyfriars Abbey, founded by Richard Fiztjohn and his wife Alice. This too is in danger from the eroding coast.

Chapter Seven

Topsham

In the 1990s we booked a holiday at Exmouth on a caravan site for my youngest daughter and myself.

We didn't particularly want to be at a holiday camp, but it was good value. We made the best of it and spent most of our time exploring the area.

Most of the holiday it rained, as it does in England. This green and pleasant land!

Our day out by taxi and train took us a few miles down the coast to a pretty part of Devon, the town of Topsham. We wandered thought the winding narrow streets on our way to the quay. Passing many small independent shops and an old book shop, I went in and brought an old book on the history of Exeter.

Near the quay are a few pubs. We visited the Steam Packet pub; this is the second oldest pub in Topsham. We had a drink and a ploughman's lunch. This consisted of cheese, pickle, lettuce, tomatoes, and a very large bread roll. The service was very good and the food was good value.

Standing on the quay we could see across the water to Powderham Castle where the Courtenay family still live.

Isabella de Fortibus, Countess of Devon and Lady of the Isle of Wight, owned Topsham. She had mills nearby, and she had a barrier put across the River Exe to make the tidal river higher at Topsham to run her mills. It was removed by Henry VIII.

Further down the estuary is the Countess Wear. This village-like parish was originally a part of Greater Topsham.

In 1844 it became a parish in its own right.

The area was named after Isabella de Fortibus. In the time of Henry III, the weir was built to power her mills. It may have been built between 1272 and 1284.

Edward IV granted permission for the weir to be breached, but it was too late: the river channel had silted up.

The Isle of Wight

I wanted to see what Isabella, Lady of the Isle of Wight, had thought when returning home from the mainland of England in middle of thirteenth century.

I knew my journey would be different as it was 2002, and I would be travelling by train and catamaran to the Isle of Wight.

She would have travelled by horse and boat, probably a sailing boat. My journey was quicker and more comfortable. I travelled on a train with all the modern conveniences of seats, toilets , a smooth ride, and air conditioning, and food was available to buy.

I started out from Northampton and changed trains at Coventry and Southampton, finally arriving at Portsmouth Harbour to wait for the catamaran to take me over to the Isle of Wight. The train journey took a total of four hours train journey, and there was also twenty minutes on the catamaran across the Solent.

It became clear why Isabella enjoyed returning home.

She must have looked at the island as they set sail from the mainland and thought, "I own all this .This is my home." She lived in Carisbrooke Castle, high on a hill overlooking all the island with Newport, the capital, not far away. It was the ideal place to build a castle to keep the enemy out and to see anyone visiting the castle.

Isabella de Fortibus

Isabella was about fifteen years old in 1248 when she was married to William de Fortibus, the Earl of Albemarle. He had been married before. His wife, Christian daughter of Allan, the Earl of Galloway, died 1246 leaving no children. In 1260 Isabella`s husband William de Fortibus died while he was on business in France. She inherited his lands in Yorkshire, and in 1262 after the death of her brother Baldwin de Redvers, she inherited the castle and other land.

Isabella had five children named .John, Thomas, William, Amicia, and Avelina.

Isabella was given personal custody of the children. For their maintenance, "Kenyngton extra Lambeth" was given to her, and also Pocklington in Yorkshire.

Her great-great-grandmother Matilda Golafre who married William de Courcy came from Northamptonshire.

It was said that Isabella was a figure of great beauty and of enormous wealth, strong character and of unbending will.

She held many estates, including Newnham in Oxfordshire, the Isle of Wight, parts of Northamptonshire, Oxfordshire, Berkshire, Bedford, Hereford, Cambridge, Norfolk, Suffolk, and Essex. She also owned Pishobury in Sawbridgeworth, Hertfordshire. This is near to where David and Victoria Beckham had a home.

The emblem used for the Vauxhall car, the griffin, was taken from Faulk de Breauté's shield. He had married Margaret Fitzgerald, widow of Baldwin de Redviers.

Margaret was grandmother to Isabella de Fortibus, the Lady of the Isle of Wight and, Countess of Devon. Her house on the south bank of the Thames was known as Fulk's hall. Later it became known as Foxhall, and eventually Vauxhall.

The famous Vauxhall pleasure gardens were created in the seventeenth century near the site of Fulk's Hall.

A Thirteenth-Century Tale

As Isabella's barge sails in the Solent from the Isle of Wight to Hampshire, the boatmen sing:

O green isle of Vectis,
The sailors love thee,
Their sweet home,
Their haven from toils of the sea.
O Vectis, green Vectis,
Thou jewel of the sea,
Though sea mists be shrouding
The shores from our sight
The heat ever holdeth
The image of Wight.
O Vectis , green Vectis,
Thou star of the night
Blow softly ye breezes
When springtime is here.
Oh! waft the sweet odours
And songs that are dear.
O Vectis , green Vectis,
Thou land without peer,
When high waves are rolling
Tween bark and our home,
Our island hath voices
That bid us to come.
O Vectis , green Vectis,
Thou call'st cross the foam.
O green isle Vectis,
Our voyage once o`er
Oh, one highest to heaven`s
Thy welcoming shore
O Vectis , green Vectis
Who wouldn't love thee
Thou gem of the ocean
The jewel of the sea.

(From a book by Sir Fred Black, County Press . Newport, Isle of Wight, 1924.
With permission from Editor of Isle of Wight County Press, December 2008.)
This poem is relevant to my journey to the Isle of Wight. It is how I imagined Isabella de Fortibus, the Lady of the Isle of Wight, saw her journey back to her island.

Carisbrooke Castle

During my second visit to the Isle of Wight, I wanted to visit Carisbrooke Castle and research the history of its occupants in Newport reference library. I was on my own. The bus dropped me at the bottom of the hill in the village of Carisbrooke. I looked up and could see the castle. I knew I had a steep hill to climb, but I was here, so there could be no going back!

I followed a group of people as they went off road. We walked through thickets and bushes, until we came to rampart walls. Then we walked alongside the walls until we came to the gate house. On entering the shop, I realised I couldn't afford to enter the castle and buy a souvenir as well. I chose a souvenir helmet key ring instead.

On being allowed to use their toilets, I gained an insight of the courtyard, As I had to walk across the courtyard, I could feel the presence of Isabella de Fortibus acknowledging the effort I had taken to get there. She was the reason that I had returned; she was a distant ancestor of the family. Could the ghost of a lady wearing a long cloak and walking with her four lap dogs be Isabella?

Isabella de Fortibus was the first person to have glass in the windows of the castle; this would have been a very great expense. She also had a chapel built in the castle grounds.

13th century window
Carisbrooke Castle
made for Isabella.

She was the wealthiest lady in the country outside the royal family.

Carisbrooke Castle is a real medieval castle and well worth a visit for the whole family. In the castle grounds there are two wells. One well is at the keep and can only be reached by climbing seventy-one steps. The one used now is in the well house in the courtyard of the castle. Donkeys work a water treadwheel to bring up the water from the well. They can still be seen today, working for a short time.

Quarr Abbey

On my first visit to the Isle of Wight on 6 September 2001, I decided to go and see Quarr Abbey. It was only a few miles from where I was staying at Ryde. The day would have been Nancy Gulliver's eighty-fifth birthday.

The day started with a light rain, but later in the day the sun came out.

A ten-minute walk to Ryde bus station and a fifteen-minute bus ride brought me to the entrance of Quarr Abbey.

I walked along a tree-lined avenue, very dark with overgrown trees and bushes shading the sunlight. The abbey was hidden from view.

I wanted to see where some of the Lords of the Isle of Wight were buried. Among those there was Baldwin de Redvers, fourth Lord of the Isle of Wight, and Cecily of York, the daughter of King Edward IV.

It was a short walk from the abbey, turning right and down a rough farm track. The monks at the abbey used this track as they kept animals in the fields. In a field overlooking the Solent stand the remains of the old Quarr Abbey. This is where some of the family of Redvers are buried. There is a wonderful view of the sea from the field, with ships passing by.

William de Redvers, brother of Baldwin de Redvers, also died at Quarr Abbey. It was his grandson, Baldwin de Redvers III, who married Amice de Clare (born 1220; died 1284) daughter of the Duke of Gloucester, and had two children, Baldwin IV and Isabella . Baldwin married Ava de Savoy from the Italian royal family and had a son John, who died as a young boy.

Isabella also married and had five children. They all died before she did.

On the death of her brother Baldwin IV, she became Lady of the Isle of Wight and Countess of Devon and owned all of the Isle of Wight and land and manors in England, including Harewood in Yorkshire. Her youngest daughter Aveline married Edmund, Earl of Lancaster, the son of King Henry I. When she was on her death bed in Lambeth London, King Edward I send men to her bedside to persuade her to sign the Isle of Wight over to him. It was exchanged for 4,000 marks. She was buried at Breamore Priory in Hampshire. There is no trace left of the priory or the burial place left.

I found a small shop housed in an outhouse near the abbey, selling books and cards and pottery. It was manned by a solitary monk, Dom Robert Gough. He had been born in Ryde on the Isle of Wight and died on the island on 30 January 2004.

Looking around the small shop, I asked the monk serving there if I could possibly go into the church and have a few minutes to pray. He unlocked the door of the church and escorted me into the church. It was empty of all but essential furniture — a place of solitude and a good place to pray and reflect on life.

Ghosts of the Isle of Wight

Over the centuries, many famous people have stayed or lived on the Isle of Wight, including Keats, Dickens, Tennyson, and Longfellow.

Queen Victoria had a home built on the island, called Osborne house, and earlier King Charles I had been imprisoned at Carisbrooke castle.

The Isle of Wight is reputed to be the most haunted island in the world. It is said that ghosts abound and the Isle of Wight has supernatural energy.

Unquiet and restless souls have been reported from hotels, hospitals, manor houses, pubs, prisons, churches, and shops.

Some of the places to visit to (maybe) experience the ghosts on the island include:

Arreton Manor (a little girl in a blue dress and a lady in red gown)

Appuldurcombe

Knighton Gorges

Northwood House

Needles Old Battery (ghosts of World War I soldiers)

The Longstone (a thirteen-foot-tall rock)

Royal Yacht Squadron (ghost of the Marquis of Anglesey who lived at Cowes Castle, died 1854)

The Prince Consort in Ryde (amorous maid)

Priory Bay Hotel in Ryde (sprit of young girl and dog)

The Hare and Hounds in Arreton (ghost of Michael Morey)

Isle of Wight Waxworks (ghost of Louis de Rochefort)

Isle of Wight Zoo in Sandown (a young soldier cut in half accidentally in 1888)

The Golden Fort (a World War I sergeant-major fell down the staircase)

Chale Church (a watcher ghost waits for next soul to be buried in the churchyard)

Ventnor Botanic Gardens, previously a hospital (phantom nurses walk round the gardens)

The Royal Essex Tearoom in Godshill (the ghost of a little black cat)

The Castle of Carisbrooke, a few miles from the capital of the island, Newport, has a number of ghosts.

In the famous well house, where the donkeys work the wooden treadwheels to draw up the water, there is the face of a long-dead girl, Elizabeth Ruffin, who drowned in the well.

Around the castle grounds there walks a figure in a long cloak with four dainty lap dogs. On the moat is a young man in a brown jerkin and trousers.

A Victorian lady in grey is felt at the castle gatehouse. I felt her presence as I entered the castle — a cold feeling.

If you enjoy the unknown and want to see a beautiful small island, then visit the Isle of Wight. Who knows what you may see!

Christchurch

This was my third visit to this town in Dorset near the New Forest. The first time was in late 1950s. My sister and I had been on holiday in Bournemouth with Aunty Nancy. We had visited Christchurch for the day. The second visit was while the family was staying in our folding caravan at Mudeford. We walked round the old market town with the castle, the constable's house, and the large priory.

The image of the priory stayed with me.

Fifty years later I walked the same route, this time with a friend of mine, David Popham, a psychotherapist.

He lived in Christchurch. He is not to be confused with David Popham the author who wrote The History of Wimborne.

I was visiting the town for the weekend and to see my friend and his dogs.

We walked around the town centre with its small quaint streets. It was very busy with lots of traffic. In the summer months it is full of holidaymakers.

In September it was warm and sunny. Most of the people walking around were elderly people who had moved there to retire and enjoy life near the sea.

A walk through the pretty grounds of the priory along the river's edge gave time for reflection among the trees and gardens. There are seats for anyone who wants to rest a while.

Within the grounds is the ruin of the castle. Nearby is the constable's or bailiff's house. This was built in 1160 for a bailiff or constable to live in when the Lord of the Manor was away on business. In Christchurch priory is a stained glass window in memory of Isabella de Fortibus, depicting her on her deathbed signing the document containing the handover of the Isle of Wight to King Edward I for 40.000 marks.

The Redvers family held Christchurch for 200 years. The last in the family was Isabella de Fortibus; her children had all died before her. She died at her home at Lambeth in London and was buried at Breamore Priory in Hampshire. No visible remains of the priory survive today.

The rivers Avon and Stour both enter the sea at Christchurch with beautiful views and a large park at the harbour entrance.

I had achieved my reason for visiting Christchurch, researching and taking photographs and to have a good few days' holiday break.

Chapter Eight

Dublin

I was lucky to be able to travel to Dublin in 2006 for my sixtieth birthday. It w
as a city I had always wanted to visit. Dublin is smaller than London and was easy to get around. The people were very friendly.

My friend from Ireland took me round the city, down o` Connell Street. It was here that the Easter Rising occurred outside of the post office. It was taken over by Irish volunteers and the Irish Citizen Army. Here guns were shot, and holes in the building still remain.

We went across the halfpenny bridge over the river Liffey to Temple Bar where we saw the cultural area of the city. The streets were full of people drinking and entertainers busking. On to Trinity College, St Patrick's Cathedral, and Marsh Library.

Jonathan Swift
St Patrick's Cathedral is a beautiful place, and monuments fill the whole of the cathedral. Many visitors walked around in amazement.

I had wanted to visit the cathedral to see where Jonathan Swift had lived and worked and was buried. He had been Dean of St Patrick's Cathedral from 1713 to 1745.

On his death, he left in his will £12,000 for the building of St Patrick's Psychiatric Hospital. He may have suffered mental health issues himself, and he had no immediate family to leave the money to.

He visited Banbury in England and stayed at the Whately Hall Hotel while he started to write his book Gulliver's Travels.

Opposite the hotel is St Mary's Parish Church. In the graveyard there are tombs containing some of the Gulliver family from the Banbury area.

Jonathan Swift had family connections with the Dryden family of Canons Ashby , Northamptonshire.

He was born in 1667 in Dublin and died in 1745. He is buried in St Patrick's Cathedral, Dublin. Marsh's Library was built next door.

His grandmother was Elizabeth Dryden, aunt of John Dryden the poet. born at Aldwinckle near

Oundle in Northamptonshire.

He may have been in the Canons Ashby area visiting his grandmother's relations. Did he get the idea of calling his book Gulliver's Travels after seeing the gravestones in St Mary's churchyard in Banbury?

Holyhead

Visiting Holyhead on a bright autumn day brought back many special memories of my childhood.

I was again travelling by train. Sitting in a comfortable seat by the window, I watched the beautiful scenery of North Wales pass by.

We were a family who always travelled by train on long journeys for our holidays. This was because my father worked on the railway as a signal and telegraph engineer. He was given a free rail travel card for his wife and children.

I had memories of our journey to Llandudno, where our parents had spent their honeymoon and we spent most of our childhood holidays. My parents had friends who moved from Blisworth, Northamptonshire to Llanfairfechan in North wales. They ran a school in the village of Llanfairfechan. Each time we had a holiday in Wales we visited them.

Their house in Llanfairfechan was built a few yards from the sandy beach, overlooking Puffin Island (Ynys Seriol in Welsh).

Their back garden was full of vegetables, ready to be picked and cooked for a meal.

At the end of the garden was gate that opened out to the Llanfairfechan railway station.

In all the world, I considered this my perfect home. You could
 walk out of the front door onto a sandy beach with wonderful views of the sea and Puffin Island.

The back gate took you straight on to the railway station.

Sadly with time this has changed.

As we travelled through the station, I could see a large metal fence blocking access from the front garden to the station platform.

On the other side of the station runs the dual carriageway (the A55) to Holyhead.

The train journey continued on towards Holyhead.

We passed by Bangor, on to the Menai Straits, Anglesey.

We crossed the Britannia Bridge built by George Stephenson. It has now been rebuilt after a fire in 1970 and is used by trains on one level and by cars and lorries on another.

We passed by a small station with the longest name –
Llanfairpwllgwyngllgogerychwyrndrobwllllantysiliogogogoch.

In English it means "St Mary's church in the hollow of the white hazel near the rapid whirlpool and the church of St Tyshio by the red cave".

The next station is called Valley and is where RAF Valley is situated. Prince William is stationed here as a search and rescue pilot.

On the horizon I could see the beautiful beaches of Anglesey.

Within a short time we had arrived on Holy Island and at Holyhead.

Most people pass through the town on their way to the harbour to board a ferry to Ireland, either the port of Dublin or Dun Laoghaire.

Jonathan Swift who wrote Gulliver's Travels and many other books, including books of poems, made this journey many times.

It would have been completely different to my journey.

He travelled on horseback with a servant and guide for company.

They travelled to Chester and onwards to Holyhead, resting at taverns or inns along their way.

They may have used the old road winding through the villages of North Wales. Princess Diana and Prince Charles travelled this road by car when they opened the art centre (now the Venue Cymru) at Llandudno in October 1981.

For parts of Jonathans Swift's life he worked for Sir William Temple of Moor Park , Surrey before he returned to Dublin and became Dean of St Patrick's Cathedral. He wrote poems while waiting at Holyhead for the calmer weather travel across the Irish Sea.

O Neptune! Neptune! must I still
Be here detain'd against my will?
Is this your justice, when I'm come
Above two hundred miles from home;
O'er mountains steep, o'er dusty plains,
Half choked with dust, half drown'd with rains,
Only your godship to implore,
To let me kiss your other shore?
A boon so small! but I may weep,
While you're like Baal, fast asleep.

Lo, here I sit at Holy head
With muddy ale and mouldy bread;
All Christian vittals stink of fish,
I'm where my enemies would wish.

Convict of lies is ev'ry sign
The Inn has not a drop of wine,
I'm fastened both by wind and tide,
I see the ships at anchor ride,
The Captain swears the sea's too rough
(He has not passengers enough).
Written by Jonathan Swift
Today it is a different view of the harbour. The harbour has been extended and modern facilities built. There are new waiting rooms and clean toilets, a fully stocked cafe with fresh packed food and drink. No sight of muddy ale or mouldy bread!

Marsh Library

The library was built by Archbishop Narcissus Marsh in 1701 and is situated next to St Patrick's Cathedral in Dublin.

It contains 25,000 books dating back to the sixteenth, seventeenth, and eighteenth centuries and maybe earlier. It was the first public library in Ireland.

Before my visit I had made arrangements via email with Muriel McCarthy. She was the keeper of the library. I was excited to visit Marsh Library, a place of great historic reference.

Some of the books are so rare and valuable that they are kept behind a wire cage. Years ago, if you wished to read them, you would have to be locked in the cage with the book by a member of staff.

I was met by Muriel McCarthy. She ordered the first edition of Gulliver's Travels to be brought out for me to see. I wasn't allowed to touch it, just to sit and look at it. It was a small book in very good condition, and I was happy just to enjoy seeing the book in front of me.

She told me that the seat where I was sitting was the seat where Bram Stoker had sat while he studied while he was a student at Trinity College. I felt really lucky to be sitting there. Stoker came to the library several times throughout 1866 while he was a student. It was relevant that I understood all about Bram Stoker. Two of my grandchildren are related to Bram Stoker though their father's paternal grandmother, Miss A. Stoker.

Chapter Nine

Jersey

A bright early morning started my day out to Jersey in 2008.

This was a trip I wanted to make – a return to Jersey in the Channel Islands, a place i had first visited in 1968. This time the journey would be on my own. I still wanted to visit the beautiful island once again.

Forty years later it still had the magic of being in a foreign country, but nearly everyone spoke and understood English. French and Jerriais language are also used on the island.

I booked a flight from Birmingham international airport using Flybe, who are part owned by British Airways. I am disabled with arthritis and cannot walk very far without a lot of pain. When I enquired if they could help me at the airport, I was pleasantly surprised to find that they could give me assistance from check-in to the airplane, via a wheel chair. Not letting my pride get the best of me, I accepted their offer. Sure enough, as I sat in the special assistance corner, an airport staff member came and took me to a minibus across the airport to the waiting plane. There were about four small steps to climb, with help from the air stewardess. I was given a seat near the front of the plane and a glass of orange. I was treated very well.

The journey over to the islands gave me a very clear view of Oxford, Christchurch, Poole, the Isle of Wight, and all the Channel Islands. I again marvelled at being able to see the land below from the plane window. It looked just like a map of the islands. This man-made metal machine was flying in the air like a bird, just below the clouds. I said a prayer of thanks for the safe journey.

A short walk through Jersey airport led to the taxi rank or the local bus stop. I chose a taxi so as to spend my short time there as best I could. I was to meet up with a lady who works in Jersey Museum in St Helier. We had corresponded by email for a few months, and she had offered to show me round the museum. I was again doing some research for my forthcoming book Gulliver Travels Again. I wanted to see Emilie le Breton's (Lillie Langtry's) possessions and travelling box that had been left to the museum after Lillie died in Monte Carlo in 1929.

Lily Langtry

Upstairs was an art gallery, which was reached via a lift or by the stairs. There were others floors in the museum to see. The artwork in the gallery included many works by the Romantics, including two portraits of Lillie Langtry. I was allowed to sit and look at them. I marvelled at the beauty of this lady. No wonder the Prince of Wales wanted her!

08/10/2008

Lillie Langtry s father's family had been born on the island of Jersey in 1853. Her maiden name was Emilie Charlotte le Breton; she did not like this name and was happy to be called Lillie.

In 1874 she married Edward Langtry. She didn't love him; it was said that she loved the yacht he owned. Marriage meant to her freedom from the island, hopefully ending up in London, where all the action seemed to go on. She began to have an affair with Queen Victoria's son, the Prince of Wales. He was married to Princess Alexandra, but he had many affairs, always with married women. While with Lillie Langtry, he would organise fishing trips with his friends and would include Edward Langtry in the party. While they were away, he had time to conduct his affair with Edward's wife, Lillie.

By 1878 Lillie was able to have her portraits painted by Sir John Everett Matthias, a fellow

Jersey man, and by Sir Edward Pointer. She now had a high circle of friends and could get credit easily.

Her relationship with the Prince of Wales came to an end, and she became friendly with Prince Louis of Battenberg. She gave birth to a daughter Jeanne. The father may have been Prince Louis, Lord Louis Mountbatten's father and grandfather of Philip, Duke of Edinburgh, or her old friend, Arthur Jones, an illegitimate son of Lord Ranelagh.

Some of the Well-Known Gullivers

George Gulliver

George Gulliver was great-great-uncle of Brian Gulliver of Wenvoe, Cardiff, Wales. He was
born in Banbury in 1804 and died in Canterbury in 1882. He was an
anatomist, a physiologist, and surgeon to Royal Horse Guards (the Blues). He wrote several books, including, A Catalogue of Plants Collected in the Neighbourhood of Banbury, 1841. He was in correspondence with Charles Darwin.

Three letters survive written between Charles Darwin and George Gulliver. Here is the transcript of one of the letters from Darwin to George Gulliver.

Down Bromley . Kent
Dec 18th

Dear Sir.

I thank you sincerely for your extremely kind letter, and for all the great trouble you have taken in explaining to me [and it was very necessary] how to send the blood. I send by this post, blood of the barb, short-faced tumbler and dragon, which latter is nearly as good as that of carrier. These are 3 very distinct breeds; unfortunately I have not one common blue chequered rock or dovecot pigeon; nor is one kept, within half a dozen miles of this place; if you could possibly get blood of this. I shall think it would be very desirable, as standard.

I shall soon have Spanish runts and turbots, and if your examination gives any hope of anything curious I would send examples of them and of fantails and pouters, and then you would have blood of every main breed. I shall be very curious to hear the result. With respect to your very kind offer of sending me the book edited by you; if you are quite sure you can spare a copy. I shall be very glad of it, for the fact stated by you of the difference in the blood of congenerous animals seems to me very curious.

I am nearly sure that the passenger pigeon and turtle dove have interbred, so that if the blood of the former differs from the latter, it is eminently curious. I have often observed that when one single character in a species differs in a marked and extraordinary degree from that of its congeners, this character is

apt to be variable, especially if several individuals from different habitats are observed; I presume that you examined the blood of only single individuals in the cases enumerated by you, in which the blood presented very marked characters; but I should be glad to hear whether you noticed any unusual variability in the corpuscles in these particular species.

I am almost sure I have read in zoolog. Proceeding an account by you of the blood of different races of dogs; and if I am right, I have certainly marked the passage, and shall meet with it again, when going over books read of late years. Nevertheless I shall be very much obliged if you would inform me, whether it has so happened that you have, since such publication,

examined the blood of any other varieties or breeds of dogs or any other domesticated animals.

I fear you will think me quite unreasonable , but I would ask whether it would not be worthwhile to look at the blood of battams, cochin-chinas, dorking or game: i.e., of 2 or 3 of the most strongly marked races or species. You will see that the kindness of your note has made me greedy in my enquires.

Pray believe me, my dear sir, with very sincere thanks.

Yours truly obliged.

Charles Darwin.

(With permission from

Stephen Keynes, Charles Darwin Trust, and Dr Alison Pearn, Cambridge University)

Charles Gulliver

Charles Gulliver was born in 1837 in Marston St Lawrence. He was a lay preacher at a Methodist church in Northants. He married Mary Heritage. They lived at West Thorp. Northamptonshire. He farmed, and she ran a beer house. They had a large family. Charles and Mary were my great-grandparents.

Harold Gulliver

Harold Gulliver lived from 1908 to 1998. He was born in Helmdon. He was a farmer, the president of Northampton Baptist Association, and the chairman of local NFU. He came from a large family. He was a cousin of my grandfather, Fred Gulliver. His father was Albert Jesse Gulliver from the Towcester area of Northamptonshire.

James Gerald Gulliver

1930–1996, born in Campbeltown, Scotland, was the son of a grocer. He was co-founder of Argyll Store, Fine Fare, and Safeway's. He bought a Scottish Island and Upper Slaughter manor house in the Cotswolds, which was opened as a hotel. Though correspondence, he invited us to look around the hotel and gardens . He was away on business when we called, and sadly we never got to meet him.

He was married four times.

Benjamin Gulliver

Ben Gulliver and his family emigrated from England, settling in Townsville, Queensland, Australia.

In the 1880s he owned land in Townsville, Queensland, and ran a successful nursery and pleasure garden. It was called Acacia Vale Nursery and Pleasure Gardens. Later the area was named after him. It is still called Gulliver.. Ben Gulliver grew and sold plants and trees to local people. He was famous for growing mangoes. Some of the many varieties of trees that he grew, still survive today.

Trevor Gulliver

Trevor Gulliver was joint owner of St John's Bread and Wine, St John's Restaurant , Spitalfields. London.

Isaac Gulliver

Isaac Gulliver was born 1745 in Semington, Wiltshire.
He lived in Dorset and Hampshire.
He was known as a lovable villain, and it is claimed he never killed anyone.
In Dorset he was known as a famous smuggler who smuggled silk, tobacco, spirits, tea, and wine.
Lots of properties in and around Bournemouth and Poole were owned by him. Many times he bought and sold his home to avoid the tax man.
One time he was supposed to have stored contraband in the tower of St Andrew's Church, Kinson, Bournemouth.
He had many people who followed him. They all wore uniforms that were of copies of smocks worn by a Dorset farm hand.

His favourite place for smuggling contraband into the country was Branksome Chine. This is now a peaceful, shaded woodland walk reaching down to a sandy beach. Canford Cliffs is near the eastern end of Poole harbour with wonderful views of the sea. All these places I have visited, and I could imagine Isaac Gulliver and his men bringing in the supplies from the ships.

Issac Gulliver married Elizabeth Beale. They had one son. Isaac, who died at the age of twenty-four, and two daughters, Elizabeth and Ann. They both married into wealthy families.

The senior Isaac Gulliver died at his home in Wimbourne and is buried beneath the central isle of Wimbourne Minister.

We spent many holidays in and around Bournemouth, Christchurch, and Poole tracing the steps that he may have taken. We visited Isaac`s last home in Wimbourne and saw the church where he is buried.

There is a district of Poole is called Lilliput . The name is used in the book Gulliver's Travels.

Final Thoughts

As I come towards the end of this long journey, I look back and remember all the people I have met on the way. Most people have been very kind and helpful, letting me see documents and lending me photographs to use that may have been have belonged to their families for years. I am grateful to them for allowing me permission to use them in my book.

I am grateful to my parents for believing in me that I could write this book, even though I have dyslexia and do not find it easy to write and spell correctly. Thank goodness for computer spell check!

I have visited many places, knowing they had some connection with the Gullivers in the past.

I have had the good fortune to the title of Lady of the Manor, a title that belonged to the Gulliver family. I can call myself Susan . Lady of the Manor of Gullivers(Golofer/Golafres).

The family lived in Little Comberton near Pershore in Worcestershire six hundred years ago.

I had always wondered why I couldn't find the name of Gulliver in the history book. Now I know that they changed the spelling of their name from a Normandy spelling of Goulafre to an English spelling of Gulliver.

Some of my journeys were by train or car or plane. Most were by train, my favourite kind of transport.

I have one more country to visit — Normandy in France. Here I will be able to see where it all began in La Goulafriere, the village that the Gullivers owned. They had changed the name of

the village from Bernard de Mesnil to La Goulafriere.
I hope to visit it one day.

References

Crisp. The Middle Ages. Toucan Publishing, 1997.
Imogen Dawson. Food and Feasts in the Middle Ages. Zoe Books, Ltd, 1994,
Tessa Hosking. Medieval Britain (Family Life). Wayford, 1994.
www.smuggling.co.uk
Stephen Keynes and Dr Alison Pearn of the. Charles Darwin Trust, Cambridge University.
Muriel McCarthy of Marsh Library, Dublin, Ireland.
Gay Baldwin. Ghost Island.
Sir Fred Black (1924). Newport, Isle of Wight Isle of Wight County Press.
Mrs Rose Troup, Lady of the Isle of Wight.
Phillip Brown. www.banburycakes.co.uk
Peter Clarke, Assistant Editor of the Chronicle and Echo.
David Saint of the Chronicle and Echo.
www.fabpedigree.com
Heralds' visitation, Northamptonshire,
Heralds' visitation, Warwickshire,
www.fawsley.com
George Baker., History of Northamptonshire. 1820.
S.S. Campion. Northampton Town Hall: Its Story Told by itself. W. Mark and Co., 1925.
The Golden Falcon website.
Richard Hart. The Vauxhall and Bedford Story. Farnon Books, 1996.
Brian Gulliver.
Susan Brown.
Birmingham Reference Library.
Felicia Hermans. The poem "The Stately Homes of England".
(Courtesy of Liverpool libraries services).
Northampton Local Studies Library,
Greyfriars.ox.ac.uk
Edward Rusby in Fyfield Parish Magazine, 1975.
The Leadenhall Market website.
David Cornforth. "Topsham — a short history" on the Exeter Memories website.
W.A. Copinger. The Manors of Suffolk: Notes on Their History and Devolution. London, Unwin, 2005.

William Page and J.W. Willis-Bund (editors). A History of the County of Worcestershire, volume 4. Victoria County History, 1924.
Mathew Lloyd. www.arthurlloyd.co.uk
The Guildhall Library, City of London.
The local history collection in the city library of Townsville, Queensland, Australia.
St John`s Restaurant. St John's Bread and Wine, London.
To all people that I haven't named. Sorry and Thank you!

Back Page

Susan Clarke lives in Northampton. She was born in 1946 at the Barratt Maternity Hospital, Northampton.

She was a junior member of the PDSA and used to help raise money for the charity

She attended St Giles Church of England Primary and Junior School. She appeared as a Japanese girl wearing a pink silk kimono at the New Theatre, Abington Street, Northampton in a play called "Make Believe", arranged by Mrs Jessie Knight of Harpole. The funds raised were in aid of charity.

At Barry Road Girls School she was introduced to William Shakespeare and Wordsworth's written work.

At Roade School she was a member of the school hockey team. They played against other schools in the county.

She attended Northampton Technical College, now the University of Northampton, where she studied dressmaking and tailoring.

At Northampton Art College she studied dress design and the history of buildings and monuments. One of her teachers was the famous local artist, Henry Bird,

The painting by Peter Newcombe shows an old farm cart that belonged to Fred Gulliver of Glebe Farm, Blisworth. It was here that my sister and myself used to play as children pretending that it was a barge on the canal. We would be amused for hours — just us and the mice and rats and the owl that lived in the barn.

The cart is now owned by Peter Newcombe.

The picture of the Palladian bridge , Stowe Gardens , Buckinghamshire is by Barry Turland.

CPSIA information can be obtained
at www.ICGtesting.com
Printed in the USA
241392LV00002B

9 781438 964867